The Inner Path

❀

An introduction to Buddhist practice for those in prison

Acharya Samaneti

The Inner Path
An introduction to Buddhist practice for those in prison
Acharya Samaneti

Published by **Sumeru Press Inc.**
PO Box 75, Manotick Main Post Office,
Manotick, ON, Canada K4M 1A2

Editing & Design: Karma Yönten Gyatso

All text and photographs were created through my years of experience as a spiritual care worker in the prison environment. All identities of residents of the various penitentiaries who inspired this book are excluded for their protection. This book is offered free of charge to all incarcerated people, pre-trial detainees, conditionally released people, and those in all situations between these stages.

ISBN: 978-1-998248-10-0

Library and Archives Canada Cataloguing in Publication

Title: The inner path : an introduction to Buddhist practice for
    those in prison / Acharya Samaneti.
Names: Samaneti, Acharya, author.
Identifiers: Canadiana 20240504445 | ISBN 9781998248100
    (softcover)
Subjects: LCSH: Buddhism. | LCSH: Prisoners—Religious life.
Classification: LCC BQ5395 .S26 2024 | DDC 294.3/444—dc23

For further information about The Sumeru Press,
please visit us at **sumeru-books.com**

Contents

More >

Introduction

What you hold in your hands is the product of my years of experience as a spiritual care worker in a prison environment. I have served people in all the penitentiaries in my region: super max, maximum, medium, and minimum. In the course of my service, I have had the privilege of meeting a wide range people and witnessing what is most admirable in human beings. I've seen people at their lowest take charge and execute incredible changes – truly inspiring and awe-inspiring transformations.

The idea for this book has been floating around in my mind for a long time; almost since my beginnings as a spiritual care worker twelve years ago. I have always found that there was a lack of a books written for you, the residents of the various penitentiaries – a book that touched on the true realities and issues of becoming a Buddhist in a penitentiary in Canada. This book is inspired by my encounters with you and people in the same situations as you, or with similar spiritual needs. You are the inspiration for this little book, a book that I hope will be useful and an important resource on your spiritual path here in the penitentiary and even after.

This is the basis of the Buddhist path, and in a context of prison reality. I hope this becomes an essential resource that you will keep with you and turn to during difficult times or simply for support. Keep in mind that there is no ONE Buddhist book that is equivalent to the Bible, Torah, or Quran. Every Buddhist book can give you insights on your path to liberation, and each offers something of value.

This book is yours; use it. Come back to it as much as you need; it can become a reference for you and also a text that can support you during difficult times. The book is based on the basic foundational teachings that make the Buddhist path, and there will also be some appendix sections at the end with suggestions for further reading, some prayers that you can add to your daily practice, Buddhist holidays that you will be able to celebrate, and some photos of Buddha – which can be cut out to give you a picture for an altar in your cell.

Thank you for your trust, and enjoy reading!

A Note about Foreign Terms

Buddhist terms come to us from Pali and Sanskrit, two languages from the time of the historical Buddha, Shakyamuni. You may have seen those terms in one or the other language, but both are correct. When the words first appear in the book, I've included their language source and equivalent in the other language. Generally speaking, Theravada countries use the Pali spelling, whereas Mahayana and Vajrayana countries use the Sanskrit spelling. Either is fine.

All Buddhist terms and concepts will include the Pali and Sanskrit versions; in Buddhism, depending on the lineage or school, the concepts are in Pali (for Theravada) and Sanskrit (Mahayana and Vajrayana).

Pali/Prakrit is much older than Sanskrit. In fact, the meaning of the word is "original" or "natural", and Sanskrit means "refined" or "modified." Seeing as how Theravada is often called "the way of the elders," it is not surprising that they use a language which is older than the newer schools of Mahayana and Vajrayana.

The Four Noble Truths

The Four Noble Truths are the teaching at the heart of Buddhism, they are the teachings that are studied by all schools and branches of Theravada, Mahayana (Chan, Zen), and Vajrayana (Shingon, Tendai, Shugendo, Tibetan). Many people believe that the essence of the Buddhist spiritual path is contained in the teaching of the Four Noble Truths. It is also believed that these were among the first teachings shared by the Buddha after his awakening. Often we say that his teaching on dukkha[1] (unsatisfactoriness; the First Noble Truth) is the setting in motion of the wheel of Dhamma (Truth; Buddhist teachings).[2]

The First Noble Truth is simple and very clear: the truth of dukkha.

Often people translate the first Noble Truth as "life is suffering", but I prefer to say that it is unsatisfactory. I

---

1 Dukkha is commonly translated as "suffering," "pain," or "unhappiness." It is an important concept in Buddhism. It refers to the "unsatisfactoriness" or "unease" of mundane life, not being at ease when driven by craving/grasping and ignorance. In Buddhism, dukkha is part of the first of the Four Noble Truths and one of the three marks of existence.

2 Dhamma, Pali. Dharma, Sanskrit. In Buddhism, Dhamma/ Dharma (capitalized) incorporates the teachings and doctrines of the founder of Buddhism, the Buddha.

find that the term suffering is too extreme and does not capture what I call anxiety of human existence, which is dukkha. Given the unsatisfying nature of life, we might find that it is filled with suffering, or that everything we experience is unsatisfying.

Birth is unsatisfying and uncomfortable, old age is uncomfortable and unsatisfying, death is difficult and frightening for many; we cannot have everything we want, so we live with an emptiness caused by this dissatisfaction. Being separated from what we love is difficult and painful, and being associated with what we don't love is difficult and unsatisfying. So, dukkha is not just physical suffering, but any dissatisfaction that we feel as human beings, which includes stress, anxiety, fear, loneliness, unease, and so forth.

The Second Noble Truth is the origin of suffering – which is attachment.

This Noble Truth teaches us that the root of all this dissatisfaction is not necessarily desire as such, but our attachment to desire. So to avoid dukkha, we must understand what causes suffering. We can condense the root cause of dukkha simply to our attachment to desires to have (cravings), desires not to have (aversion), and ignorance of how reality actually works.

We all have likes and dislikes, and since we cannot satisfy all our wants and desires, we experience the effects of dukkha (mental disturbances and anger, which is simply another manifestation of dukkha). We must not deny our desires because that is to deny life itself. We must never fall into extremes; the real problem is that when the desire appears, we do not know it and cannot put an end to it. It is in these moments that the object of our attachments becomes a poisonous prison.

The Third Noble Truth is that cessation of our dissatisfaction is possible.

This Noble Truth teaches us that if we want to free ourselves from dukkha, we must cut off attachment. This sounds difficult, but non-attachment can be achieved through meditation practice. This freedom from attachment, from pain, frees the mind from all troubles and worries – the realization of this liberation which we called Nibbana.[3]

The Fourth Noble Truth is the path to freedom from dukkha.

We believe that Enlightenment is a condition that can be achieved by following the "eightfold path," a progressive path toward ultimate self-realization.

1. Right View or vision
2. Right Thought or intention
3. Right Speech
4. Right Action
5. Right Livelihood or fair means of existence
6. Right Effort
7. Right Awareness or attention
8. Right Concentration or meditation

---

3 Nibbana, Pali. Nirvana, Sanskrit.

The Noble Eightfold Path

As we have seen with the Four Noble Truths, the Buddha offers us a structured path which naturally guides us towards the realization of our spiritual awakening, Nibbana. This is accomplished through liberation from our attachments and illusions, and this therefore helps us understand the innate truth of all things. In Buddhism, we place great emphasis on the application of the teachings because our liberation can only be achieved through practice and not through rational understanding alone.

The path is divided into three sections which contain all eight topics that will be presented. It is divided into sections on wisdom, ethics, and meditation. The "wisdom" section includes Right Viewpoint or vision and Right Thought or intention; the "ethics" section includes Right Speech, Right Action, and Right Livelihood; the "meditation" section includes Right Effort, Right Attention, and Right Concentration.

The noble eightfold path proposed by the Buddha involves our commitment to:

1 – Right View or right vision

What we call "views" are the set of our beliefs, our mental associations and our internal thought patterns, which together are our vision of life and which condition us in the face of our decisions, our aspirations and our actions. One of the first things to do as a

Buddhist is to let go of our "points of view," at least let go enough to hold them lightly, if we want to be able to grow and have a more global vision of life around us. Our beliefs, or our frozen attachment to our beliefs, can create a lot of rigidity which will then give rise to suffering when we encounter different beliefs, and also prevent us from seeing the beliefs of others with wisdom or compassion.

Traditionally, right view is what connects the two components of Buddhism, namely doctrine and practice. Our right vision will therefore begin with an intellectual understanding of the Four Noble Truths, then be practiced concretely by beginning to "see the dukkha" in our lives, the impermanence, and the emptiness of all things. This leads to the awareness that nothing is more responsible for our suffering and attachment than wrong views, and that nothing is more productive of beneficial states and happiness than right views.

2 – Right Thought or intention

Right thinking is thinking that is unconditioned, free, without greed, jealousy, anger, hatred and cruelty. I find that the most important thing is our intention, which determines whether our words and actions will create good or bad karma.

Right thinking is not dogmatic or rigid thinking, but it is more a thought that is the expression of right understanding, of an awakened mind. So, it is a thought which is the expression of our heart, of compassion and kindness. Right intention comprises three main aspects: the intention to renounce desires, the intention to renounce anger and violence, and the intention to renounce ignorance.

3 – Right Speech

Right speech is one of the things I find most difficult because it is something we are engaged with almost all the time, so can we bring it under the influence of our spiritual practice? Not always easy or obviously, at least for me.

So what exactly does it mean to have positive speech? The Buddha asks us to refrain from telling lies, avoid attacking someone's reputation, avoid speaking hatefully, avoid speaking rudely, avoid frivolous speech or futile chatter such as gossip. Right speech allows us to speak in a noble, true and authentic way that creates harmony.

4 – Right Action

Right action is directly linked to right intention and right speech. It means we act with respect for others and for ourselves, while avoiding creating suffering for others and for ourselves. Right action is therefore action which respects the precepts, and which respects the expression of awakening. Right action, to put it simply, means acting in perfect harmony with the present moment and without ego, being completely detached from outcomes, and not seeking credit for what is achieved.

In summary, we do not act out of our own ego, and we do not act to take credit or reward for a "good" action; we act appropriately in the present moment with what best represents a free spirit filled with wisdom and compassion.

Right action is the basic precept that we must follow as Buddhists, this helps us progress on the path of the Five Precepts: refrain from killing, refrain from stealing, refrain from lying, refrain from irresponsible sexual activity, and abstaining from intoxicants. Right action is there to help us truly advance our practice and cultivate kindness and compassion towards all beings no matter who (this includes guards and all people who may represent difficulties in our lives).

5 – Right Livelihood, or fair means of existence

The Buddha advises us to earn a living righteously, without resorting to illegal and heinous activities. Our work must not come from activities based on the suffering of other beings such as killing, stealing and selling stolen property, fraud, trafficking in weapons or human beings (pimping), selling poisons or drugs, or other illegal activities.

I know this may seem difficult, because when you get out you are going to have to find a job as part of your exit plan. I say that trying to find a service or helping job is always a good guide in our job choices. It doesn't always have to be service work like spiritual care, and so on. Working in construction is a job that meets the criteria very well too because we work to build housing so that someone feels sheltered from the elements and feels safe. But yes, working in bars is not a job that aligns with this because we know all the addiction and suffering that is present in these places.

6 – Right Effort

This is the effort to apply the teachings of Buddha, the effort to work on oneself in order to improve oneself and free oneself from dukkha. We can see every action as an opportunity for self-realization that is favorable for our liberation. It is important to add a bit of nuance here. We must always remain vigilant, because if one's efforts are made selfishly, with the aim of achieving a result for oneself, the practice risks turning into a quest for profit which will be contrary to our liberation – we must always act for the good of all living beings and not just ourselves. I often remind myself that if I strive to be a better person, it is for the good of all living beings, because my actions impact and touch everyone.

7 – Right Attention or awareness

Right attention with meditation is the source of awakening and our liberation. Right attention can also be called "mindfulness". This consists of being fully alive, fully in the present moment, and not getting lost in our thoughts and stories, in anticipation or worry, in the past or the future. It is the awareness of things, of oneself, one's body, one's emotions, one's thoughts and everything around us. Also, being fully aware, fully present, means stopping judging, making categories and attaching yourself to your opinions and points of view.

Just focusing on the present moment is very beneficial for our mind – because it loses its attachments and stops its desires to have and accumulate.

8 – Right Concentration or meditation

This is fundamentally the correct practice of meditation because that is the only way to achieve the right concentration. In fact, there are several types of Buddhist meditation, with different objectives, emphasized in different traditions. Right concentration is the most important of all aspects in the noble eightfold path because without the practice of meditation, Buddhism can become just a kind of shallow intellectual juggling.

Right meditation is characterized by abandonment of the three poisons – ignorance, greed and anger, then all harmful states and conditioned states. It is founded on a return to the present moment, detachment from the everyday mind and thoughts, and transcendence of personal consciousness.

So, here is the essence of Buddhist practice explained with the noble eightfold path. This is the Truth presented to us by the Buddha; it teaches us that we can achieve complete liberation by following this simple path.

Dukkha

Dukkha is an important concept in Buddhism. I would even say that it is one of the first concepts that we learn about (I mean, it is the basis for the First Noble Truth). It's true that when I talk about dukkha during my groups or our conversations, I'm talking about dukkha simply (dukkha can be taught as a general concept, and it is often taught as a general understanding of life's difficulties); but the Buddha presented us with three kinds of dukkha because we experience this dissatisfaction at various levels. We experience dukkha first, but there are three types of dukkha in this experience:

1. *dukkha dukkha* – ordinary suffering
2. *viparinama dukkha* – suffering due to change
3. *sankhara dukkha* – suffering revealed through training

Ordinary suffering is experienced outside of meditation too. There are two types of attention – ordinary attention and attention capable of understanding the true nature of phenomena (bhavanamaya). Examples of this type of dukkha are pain, itching, irritation, any illness or physical suffering. Others could be unhappiness, sadness, pain, worry or any mental suffering.

The pain of change is experienced when we meditate with our backs straight, our legs crossed, and we try to maintain attention on the breath with determination; over time the pleasant feeling gives way to the unpleasant. Here is an example of the suffering of change. Pain appears in the back, buttocks, knees, ankles, either in the form of hardness, numbness, tingling, and so on. We notice these unpleasant sensations; they intensify, and we see them clearly. At the beginning of our practice, our patience is not developed enough, and we want to move. It is important to remember that the desire to move can decrease if we are patient. If it does not decrease over time (try to wait a little before), one can move very carefully, and the pain might decrease. Then, after some time, the pleasant again gives way to the unpleasant in the form of pressure, pain, pulsations, etc. and this time we are trying to show even more determination. Someone who is a non-practitioner or a complete beginner is unaware of the existence of these unpleasant feelings and unconsciously changes their posture. This is often because these people do not understand that the body is impermanent (*anicca*), unsatisfactory (*dukkha*) and insubstantial (*anatta*).

The Buddha taught us that there are two realities: the conventional reality (a man, a woman, a bhikkhu,[4] etc.) and the reality of the body and matter which is only understood through vipassana.[5] There is no permanent entity within us, only spirit and matter in continual flux. So, with each sensory contact, there is

---

4 A monk. Bhikkhu, Pali. Bhikshu, Sanskrit.

5 Insight meditation. Vipassana, Pali. Vipashyana, Sanskrit.

change. To be able to see this clearly and completely requires that we have practiced diligently for some
time. So, when we meditate and observe the breath
(abdomen, etc.) we must also be able to carefully observe and note all new sensory contacts: seeing, hearing, smelling, tasting, touching, or thinking. At first,
we only see the prominent sensation of the abdomen
rising and falling. Over time we see the beginning and
the whole cycle in successive phases until the end.
When we pay deep attention, we see that the abdomen (for example) does much more than just rise and
fall. With experience, we can even observe sensations
of softness, tension, pressure, and so on. These sensations too are no longer only observed in the abdomen during formal meditation – but for every sensory contact. Thoughts and emotions are also perceived
from their very beginning; this comes with time and
practice. But over time our attention becomes un-
interrupted. This is why we call it suffering revealed
through training. Our trust and faith in the dhamma
develop. Our contact with this teaching of dukkha allows us to become a better person and a freer person.

Dukkha is an important teaching, and it helps
us to see the possibilities of liberation with our deeper understanding of this essential teaching to the
Buddhist path.

Karma

What exactly is karma?

Karma is a term and concept that predates the Buddha. It has been used in various Indian religions and the most common translation of the term is "action." But, when the Buddha referred to the term karma, it was the cause of the action – the intention – and the effects. During the night of his enlightenment, the Buddha understood that all beings are born and die according to their karmic conditioning, which means that the intentions that lead to action determine what happens because of those causes: the outcome and the impact of the action. We could say it is how action moves through space and time. It was also during this night that he saw all of his past lives that went back eons, and he appreciated that the actions he had taken in his past lives propelled him into the next lives.

The Buddha taught us that although we all have accumulated karma from our past lives (including the present), karma is changeable. Every moment is an opportunity to take positive action: to think, speak and act in a skillful way that will move us away from the attachment and illusion that keeps us in suffering and *samsara*.[6] In other words, we can work and purify our karma to ensure healthier results and a better future.

---

6 The world of delusion.

Karma can still be a principle that is very useful in this life, so even if we do not believe in rebirth, this principle of karma is at the heart of the Four Noble Truths of the Buddha and his path of practice (the Eightfold Path). Even if someone does not expect to be reborn or enlightened, if the person lives virtuously and uses the logic of karma, that person and the people around them will benefit. In short, karma does not only have an impact in future lives (even if it does when we believe in rebirth). The impact is immediate in this life.

Do Buddhists believe in a God?

Since we grow up in a Judeo-Christian society, the idea of a God is fundamental to our view of religion. Because of this, it is very common for me to be asked the question "Do Buddhists believe in a god?" The quick answer is no, Buddhists do not believe in God (the Judeo-Christian god or any other god).[7] Many people believe that Buddhists consider the Buddha to be a god, but this is false. The Buddha, Siddhartha Gautama, is a person who achieved enlightenment and passed on to us the teachings that we follow to this day. The Buddha is not a god, although we may think so when looking at an altar or temple. The image of the Buddha is used to remind us of our Buddha nature and our possibility of enlightenment in this life.

Buddhists don't believe in God for several reasons. I will name a few of them, since the reasons can change depending on the country or the school.

---

7   So, what is the difference between God and a god? A deity, or "god" (with lower case g), refers to a supernatural being. Monotheism (Abrahamic religions like Christianity, Judaism, and Islam) is the belief that there is only one deity, referred to as "God" (with uppercase g). God in the Abrahamic traditions is called the Creator, because it is believed that God brought all things to life out of nothing. Comparing or equating other entities to God is viewed as idolatry in monotheism and is often strongly condemned.

These reasons are quite often shared throughout the Buddhist world.

The Buddha believed that the concept (or creation of God) came from a place of fear. Humans found themselves in a dangerous and difficult world, where predators and natural elements always threatened danger and death. So, humans created God to celebrate pleasant and joyful times – and to give the strength to continue during difficult times. I am sure that you have already witnessed people who become more religious during difficult times (in prison it is common for people to become more religious during their sentences) to give themselves the strength to get through the difficulties they experience.

The Buddha also did not believe in God because he did not find that there was sufficient proof in the texts and sermons given by the religions of his time. Every religion believes that they have the word of God in their texts, and that only they know the true nature of God. Every religion claim to have the one true proof of the existence of God but finds every other conception or proof false. A Buddhist will suspend judgment on the existence of God until irrefutable evidence is presented. In that sense, Buddhists are agnostic.

The Buddha also did not believe in God because he did not find belief in God necessary; many people will tell us the opposite because its existence gives us the creation of the universe – but science has already explained it to us completely. Thanks to this scientific explanation, we do not need to insert this idea of God as creator. We can live a useful, happy, and meaningful life without believing in God. The Buddha believed that humans had the ability to purify the mind, develop infinite love, compassion and a perfect understanding of the universe. In fact, whether there is a Creator God is irrelevant to Buddhist practice. Buddhism teaches us how to become enlightened or liberated through our own deepening understanding and efforts.

So, the Buddha is not a god, but an aspiration for us, which is why we pay homage to him – a reflection of our true nature. We do not believe in a creator, a destroyer, or an external being who sits in judgment of us; we believe in the accumulation of positive and negative karma. The other Buddhas and Bodhisattvas[8] you may have already seen (Medicine Buddha, Green Tara, and so on) are then the human form of our true nature – for example, Green Tara is a feminine manifestation of our nature of pure compassion.[9]

This question is normal. Before I educated myself and studied Buddhism, I always thought that Buddha was a god for Buddhists. I needed to put everything in terms that made sense to me; then the Buddha statue was like the crucifix at the front of the church. The important thing is that we always take the time to seek out the right information to ensure that we do not confuse the truth with our assumptions.

---

8 Buddhas in training.

9 These meditation deities are common in Mahayana and Vajrayana Buddhist traditions, but not so much in Theravada traditions.

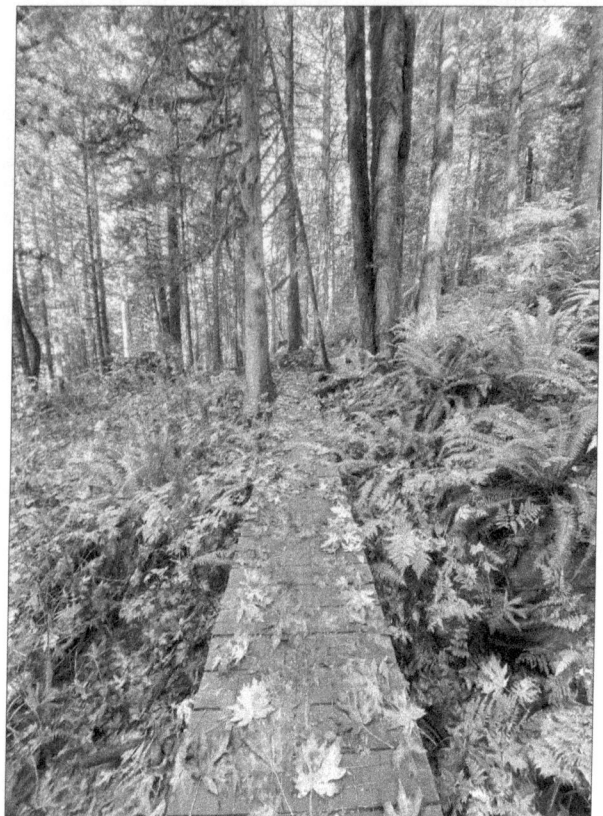

The Three Marks of Existence

The Three Marks of Existence is a teaching that is an important part of the foundation of Buddhism and is present in all the schools and the traditions. You may have seen this teaching also called the three seals of existence or the three seals of the Dhamma; it is all the same fundamental teaching – a teaching which refers us to three intrinsic characteristics of human existence.

These three perspectives describe what the nature of the perceived world looks like and all the phenomena that occur there. Understanding this triad provides the foundation for personal liberation. So, beyond just understanding the three marks intellectually, but we must also integrate them fully and authentically on an emotional level, always consistent with our attitude and behavior. I would say that most of the problems that bother us are linked to our non-acceptance of the three marks of existence. This is why we are confused, disoriented and lost.

So, what are the three marks of existence?
1. Impermanence (*Anicca*)
2. Inconsistency of an I (*Anatta*)[10]
3. Suffering (*Dukkha*)

---

10 Anatta, Pali. Anatman, Sanskrit. The other terms, Anicca and Dukkha, are spelled the same way in both languages.

The first mark is a teaching of critical importance; as the Buddha said, "everything is impermanent." Everything has a beginning and an end, nothing lasts forever or is permanent, everything passes. Everything is constantly changing, and that is why calm, and stability can only be an illusion. Everything that exists inside and outside of us is dynamic. All realities are born, live, die, and are reborn transformed to begin a new cycle. This means that who we are today is not the same as who we were yesterday. We never put our feet in the same river because the current makes the water flow constantly; there is nothing in this world that is not dynamic and constantly changing. So, it is true with us too.

The second mark teaches us that "all is without substance." This mark is what many people struggle with at the beginning of the Buddhist path. This mark means that nothing exists on its own, and nothing occurs independently. Everything that is and everything that happens is linked to multiple circumstances, factors, and facts. Thich Nhat Hanh, a famous Vietnamese Buddhist teacher, calls this Interbeing. There are connections between everything that exists. This is why, when we speak of the individual, we refer to the absence of a true "me" or "ego". As we saw with the first mark, everything is constantly changing – so a fixed identity is a false idea. We are something dynamic and transforming every moment. Our existence is a series of things heading towards their disappearance. This mark of existence encourages us to forget ourselves and not worry about the ego. What is important is that we are awake to the present moment completely. It is not important who we were yesterday and who we will be tomorrow; what is important is the action of this moment – the present moment.

The third mark, as already explained, is dukkha – "everything is unsatisfactory." You have probably already read or heard that no one can generate constant and permanent satisfaction. When you think about it, for Buddhists, what generates happiness is probably the cause of subsequent suffering. All things are victims of impermanence, even the causes of our happiness and pleasures; if we are not able to accept the first mark of existence – we will always suffer when the good times or sensations end. As the saying goes, "Good news, everything is impermanent. Bad news, everything is impermanent."

The Three Jewels

One of the oldest ways to express one's commitment to Buddhism is to take refuge in the Three Jewels. You may have heard of the Triple Gem or the Three Treasures. These terms all refer to the Buddha (the example), the Dhamma (the teachings) and the Sangha (the community of practitioners). Buddhists may recite the three vows of refuge during many rituals and ceremonies in their communities, their individual daily recitation practices, taking refuge thus:

I take refuge in the Buddha.
I take refuge in the Dhamma.
I take refuge in the Sangha.

For many practitioners, taking refuge is one of the first steps in declaring themselves a Buddhist, in addition to taking up the precepts, the guidelines for ethical living. But what is it like to take refuge in the three jewels?

Taking refuge is a way of formally expressing one's commitment to the path of the Buddha and sheltering oneself from the vicissitudes of life. When we take refuge, we do not withdraw from life; rather, it allows us to embrace the world in all its complexities as a vehicle for breaking free from our destructive bad habits. Chögyam Trungpa Rinpoche described it as "committing yourself to freedom." When we take refuge in the Buddha, we see him as a teacher and an example to follow – an ordinary person who has awakened to the human condition and who serves as our guide to a more enlightened life. In short, when we also take refuge in our own Buddha nature and our own potential for liberation.

The Buddha of refuge is not only the historical person (Shakyamuni), who had an awakening under the Bodhi tree, but also all the Buddhas whose teachings tell us that they preceded him and who will follow him, the entire pantheon of Buddhas, Bodhisattvas, and Mahasattvas[11] who are considered teachers on earth and other worlds.

The word Dhamma has several meanings, but in the Theravada, it refers to the teachings of the historical Buddha. In the Mahayana and Vajrayana traditions, the word Dharma also includes teachings of other enlightened beings. Some would say that taking refuge in the Dhamma can also mean finding support in the universe that is both visible and perfectly complete.

The Sangha is the Buddhist community. Traditionally it referred to the community of ordained monks and nuns, but today the sangha includes all Buddhist practitioners (like you), lay and ordained. Some believe that taking refuge in the sangha means embracing kinship with all living beings.

The Buddha teaches us that we are each individually responsible for our spiritual journey and our

---

11 Great practitioners.

awakening. "Be a light to yourself" is what he said to Ananda (one of his attendants) when he was dying. However, the Buddha left us a precious legacy: the teachings (Dhamma) and the community (Sangha). The teachings say that we are never alone if we take refuge in the three jewels.

We can take refuge once, on special occasions (Vesak,[12] for example), or we can do it every day. This will depend on our practice and how we want to maintain a connection with this vow of the Three Jewels. I leave you a refuge, in Pali and English, in case you want to integrate it into your spiritual practice at the intensity of your choice.

---

12 Celebrated on the Full Moon Day in May. In the Theravada, Mahayana, and Vajrayana traditions, it commemorates the Buddha's birth, enlightenment and death.

Taking Refuge

namo tassa bhagavato arahato samma-sambuddhassa
namo tassa bhagavato arahato samma-sambuddhassa
namo tassa bhagavato arahato samma-sambuddhassa
    Homage to him, the Perfect One, the Joyous
    One, the Awakened One

buddham saranam gacchami
    I go for refuge to the Buddha.
dhammam saranam gacchami
    I go for refuge to the Dhamma.
sangham saranam gacchami
    I go for refuge to the Sangha.

dutiyampi buddham saranam gacchami
    I go for refuge to the Buddha for the second time.
dutiyampi dhammam saranam gacchami
    I go for refuge to the Dhamma for the second time.
dutiyampi sangham saranam gacchami
    I go for refuge to the Sangha for the second time.

tatiyampi buddham saranam gacchami
    I go for refuge to the Buddha for the third time.
tatiyampi dhammam saranam gacchami
    I go for refuge to the Dhamma for the third time.
tatiyampi sangham saranam gacchami
    I go for refuge to the Sangha for the third time.

The Five Precepts

The precepts are an integral part of the moral practice of Buddhism. We follow these principles to ensure that we live a righteous life, cultivating habits that do not cause us to accumulate bad karma through our daily actions. By following these precepts, we also ensure that we reduce evil in our actions, thoughts and words; compassion is born from the dust of our moral practice – for these simple rules cultivate compassion with its focus on respect, generosity, truth, kindness, and discipline.

The precepts are a practice in themselves, so they are not rules that are static and unalterable (as I always understood the commandments when I was a Christian); we work on them every day. We observe how we understand them at any moment and how our experience can change our relationship to certain precepts. We can always continue to deepen our understanding and it can change over time. Sometimes I will work on a certain precept, and let it become my practice for a period of time to deepen my understanding, and also my relationship with myself and my own moral practice.

The first precept is not to kill and respect life; one must not kill a living being – more specifically, one must not intend to take the life of another living being.

The second precept is not to steal; respect for the property of others is essential in our moral practice. We must not forget that theft can be direct, that it is we ourselves who have the intention and the desire to appropriate the property of another, either by force or through deception, but it can also be indirect through others.

The third precept is not to engage in sexual misconduct. This could involve sexual assault, adultery, or sex with a person placed under the protection of a parent or with someone who is already married or in a relationship. One can be addicted to sex just as one is addicted to alcohol or gambling. These are expressions of greed, violence, and the objectification of others.

The fourth precept is not to tell lies; you must be honest. Lying is not tolerated, and distorting the truth is considered lying. This precept invites us to give a sacred value to words, because truthfulness is a source of confidence – also, false speech is that which has its roots in greed, hatred or fear, or frivolous gossip.

The fifth precept is not to use intoxicants, to have respect for a clear mind. The consumption of drugs or alcohol is prohibited. This is because consumption causes a loss of awareness. This is why Buddhists are in favor of the practice of meditation, because it is the essential means to achieve liberation (meditating under the effects of drugs or alcohol is almost impossible).

Some encourage total abstinence from drugs and alcohol, while others encourage moderation and abstinence from excess that results in intoxication.

The factors that determine whether a precept is violated have been defined in the comments below. The precept is violated only if all the conditions mentioned below are met. If one is not, the precept is still intact. If one has violated one or more precepts, one must repeat them with the firm intention of not violating them again in the future.

Taking the Precepts

1

panatipata veramani sikkhapadam samadiyami.
I strive to observe the precept of not killing.[13]

2

adinnadana veramani sikkhapadam samadiyami.
I strive to observe the precept of not taking what has not been given to me.

3

kamesu micchacara veramani sikkhapadam samadiyami.
I strive to observe the precept not to commit adultery.

---

13 Do not kill refers to any living thing, including insects.

4

musavada veramani sikkhapadam samadiyami.
I strive to observe the precept of not lying.[14]

5

sura meraya majja pamadatthana veramani
sikkhapadam samadiyami.
I strive to observe the precept of not using alcohol or
drugs that lead to neglect.[15]

---

14 Not lying also includes not backbiting, not swearing and not
talking about unnecessary things.

15 Alcohol refers to: champagne, wine, beer, pastis, whiskey and
others. Drugs: opium, cannabis, LSD, ecstasy, cocaine and
others. Cigarettes and medications containing alcohol are not
included.

Metta

The word Metta has many different meanings: loving-kindness, friendship, kindness, goodwill, harmony, gentleness and non-violence. Often in Buddhist teachings we use the word "kindness," but it is important to know that it is more than that. Simply put, it is to desire the well-being and happiness of others. The essence of Metta is an altruistic attitude of love and friendship instead of putting our personal interests first. If we have a good practice of Metta, we will refuse to be offensive and we will not have bitterness, resentment or animosity; instead, we develop a caring and generous spirit to bring well-being and happiness to others. Metta has no personal interest; it arouses warm, sympathetic, and kind feelings that can develop limitlessly with practice. Metta is universal, unconditional (we do not act out of personal interest), and total love.

With the practice of Metta, we become a source of well-being and security for others; like a mother gives her life for her child, the Metta always gives without asking anything in return. It's true that people say that it's human nature to preserve our interests. So, when this primary selfish instinct is transformed into a desire to promote the good and happiness of others, the mind becomes more expansive by identifying our own interest with the interest of all. Attitude change at the same time develops our own well-being in the best possible way.

Metta is like the protective and very patient attitude of a mother who bears difficulties out of love for her child and who protects the child all the time. Metta is also the attitude of the person who wants to offer everything that is best for his or her friend. If our Metta practice is well developed, we can develop a great inner strength that preserves, protects and heals us, as well as the people who benefit from it.

We believe that Metta is the only constructive way to bring harmony, peace and understanding between people (this could even apply to relations between people or religions, and so on.). Like most major religions, Buddhism believes that Metta is the supreme means because it constitutes the fundamental principle and basis of all benevolent activities aimed at promoting the good of human beings. When asked about his religion, His Holiness the Dalai Lama is well-known to have replied: "My religion is kindness." You don't need to be Buddhist to practice loving-kindness.

If you want to know how to practice Metta during your meditation, you can look at the "How to meditate (more experienced)" section. I recommend incorporating this focus when you have an established meditation practice.

The Aggregates

One of my first teachers once told me that we can find all the teachings of the Buddha in the Four Noble Truths; this is usually the first teaching that people study in Buddhism and it is the most important. If all the teachings are woven into the Four Noble Truths, I am often asked where I would place the aggregates then?

The *khandhas*[16] are defined as collections, groupings, or aggregates. In Buddhism we say they refer to the five aggregates of clinging – the five material and mental factors that take part in the rise of craving and clinging. I will often refer to the first Noble Truth, the truth of dukkha, to where I see the aggregates most easily.

The first Noble Truth is often translated as "life is suffering." I find that a little too simple and even a little misleading. I believe the Buddha probably would not have said suffering but dukkha instead, and it can be viewed from three different perspectives:

1. as ordinary suffering – old age, illness, death, and so on: our body, our "envelope" is bound by conditions.
2. as suffering caused by change: happy life is not eternal, permanent, and so on.

---

16 Khandhas, Pali. Skandhas, Sanskrit.

3.   as a conditioned state: our attachment to the five
     aggregates.

The first aggregate is matter, which includes the four
elements: earth [solidity], water [fluidity], fire [heat],
and air [movement], and the derivatives of the elements. When we talk about derivatives, we mean our
five sense organs (eye, ear, nose, tongue, and body)
and the external objects that correspond with the
senses:

- shapes visible to the eye;
- sounds heard by the ear;
- odors smelled through the nose;
- flavors tasted by the tongue;
- tangible things for the body;
- also all ideas, thoughts or conceptions which be-
  long to the domain of mental objects.

The second aggregate is that of sensations; this is the
group of all the pleasant, unpleasant or neutral sensations that we have during our contact between the
physical and mental organs with the outside world.
Then this includes the sensations which are born from
the contact of: the eye with visible forms, the ear with
sound, the nose with odors, the tongue and tastes, the
body and tangible objects, and the mind with mental
objects.

The third aggregate is perceptions, which, like sensations, are also of the six kinds. They are the result of
the relationship of the six interior faculties with the six

objects of the external world. It is the perceptions that recognize and interpret physical or mental objects.

The fourth aggregate is mental formations, which includes all volitional acts, good or bad: what we generally know as "karma." The Buddha defined karma as the volition of actions through the body, speech, and mind. Volition is defined as a mental construct, a mental activity – and the function is to direct the mind in the sphere of good, bad or neutral actions. We still have our basis of the six faculties and the corresponding external phenomena. Sensations and perceptions are not volitional acts. Attention, will, determination, confidence, concentration, wisdom, energy, desire, hatred, ignorance, vanity, and self-concept are.

The fifth aggregate is consciousness, which has the six faculties as its basis and the corresponding external phenomena as its objects. So, consciousness is a response or knowledge. It does not have the capacity to recognize a particular object as such – it is only the awareness of the presence of the object. For example, when your eye sees the blue of your sweater, your consciousness does not recognize that the color is blue (it has no recognition at this stage), it is the third aggregate of perception which recognizes and identifies the color like blue. Consciousness is only the knowledge of sensory experience arising from moment to moment at the gates of the senses.

So our attachment to this label that we like to give our-selves of "individual" or "person" or "I", this combina-tion of our attachment to the five aggregates, creates this deep illusion that we experience. We must not forget that they are impermanent (like all things in this world) and constantly changing, and this is why they are the cause of dukkha. We have no immutable substance or essence that can be called "I" in the five aggregates and not even outside of them. The Buddha said that everything impermanent was dukkha.

Then, as the five aggregates are born, grow, decay, and die at every moment, you yourself are born, grow, decline, and die at every moment. It is your attach-ment to this illusion created by the five aggregates that creates the dukkha you experience at every moment of your days and your life.

The Wave

Rebirth is a fundamental part of Buddhism, but often people will say reincarnation instead. I'm sure you've heard someone say that if you're not a good person in this life you'll be reincarnated as a dog in your next life; it's almost explained as a punishment for our bad deeds. I even had a guy who came to participate in my Buddhist group so that he could be reincarnated into a next life filled with luxury and comfort. (Unfortunately for him, I informed him of the motivations that we must have on the Buddhist path, and that our future happiness is not its ephemeral pleasures which is one of the roots of our suffering).

I think people will often confuse this more Hindu doctrine of reincarnation with the Buddhist perspective of rebirth; Hindus believe in *Atman* (the Self) while Buddhists believe in the idea of *Anatman* (the non-Self). For Buddhists, since everything is without an independent nature itself, they propose the concept of aggregates of attachment instead of an eternal, unchanging soul and the body as separate. We are sets of different phenomena; this attachment insists on the fact that these constituents are taken for a being which means that this attachment leads us to attach ourselves to the idea of the ego. Rebirth allows for growth and transformation, which is a good thing!

There is a continuity because death does not mean that the conditioning ends. Samsara forms a cycle of lives which follow one after the other according to the law of causality. It is therefore not the individual (the self) who continues from life to life, but rather the cosmos manifesting a different continuity. One of the best explanations I have heard is the example of the wave.

We see a wave in the ocean, we see its shape, the sun reflecting as it comes out of the ocean to fall on the beach, then just to be pulled back into the ocean. The water that was part of the wave returned to the ocean where it will manifest again in various phenomena, perhaps like a wave, but also like other things. So, the water in the wave is back. That wave will never be the same again – but it will always be made of water that is in the ocean. Rebirth is another aspect of our interbeing.

It is this continuity that the Buddha mentions during the First Noble Truth – our human birth is precious because it presents us with the possibility of transcending this cycle of existence. Understanding that we are all connected in this way also gives us the motivation to practice metta. What's good for others is good for us too because we are all in this together.

The Five Obstacles

The five obstacles are negative states of mind that can harm our Buddhist practice. They are often described as obstacles in meditation. We get to know them all very well and can experience them every day during our formal practice and in our daily activities. For each obstacle we have one or more antidotes; thanks to them, we can combat obstacles that may seem insurmountable at times.

The five obstacles are sensual desire, ill will, laziness, restlessness and doubt.

Sensual desire includes the body's appetites for food, sex, possessions, experiences. All these desires can cloud the mind and make practice much more difficult, if not impossible. The Buddha, in one of his many metaphors for obstacles, refers to sensory desire as a dye that stains a pool of clear water. Clear water reflects the face of the observer, which represents the mind which is at ease. Water stained by dye is clouded.

The antidote to sensual desire is to think about the impermanence of objects and things. All things are inherently impermanent: things come together, last for a while, then change/die. We see this with our bodies, our possessions, and even our friends and other people around us. So, if you're still overwhelmed by desires, take a moment to look at what's making you unfulfilled. Why always want new things? Are you dissatisfied with your life? Only when we get to the root of our desires can we begin to change.

Ill will refers to all aggressive states of mind – anger, hostility, resentment, bitterness. The Buddha described the mind captured by bad will as water that foams and boils. It is not calm.

The antidote to ill will is to think about compassion for others. The source of our ill will is that we see others as different from us, as separate from us. We become blind to the interconnectedness of life. We must never forget that everyone is the same, even animals; when we see that others are no different from us, we begin to develop compassion towards them – we will at least be empathetic towards them. This is how we are going to stop aggression.

Laziness is a slow and sleepy mind. A dull and sleepy mind cannot see things as they are. The Buddha compares it to a pool of water covered with moss and algae.

The antidote for laziness is quite simple. We can open our window and let some air in, take a walk in the yard, splash water in our face, meditate while standing, have a coffee, for example. It is our choice how we will do it. The important thing is to wake up and become more alert. We can also wonder what the cause of our laziness is: boredom, illness, and so on. We can think a little to find the causes of our laziness. Recognizing the causes can open up creative space for us.

Agitation captures many common feelings, such as worry, fear, or anxiety. The restless mind is disturbed and preoccupied, not ready to learn or grow.

The Buddha compares the restless mind to a pool stirred by the wind into ripples and waves.

This obstacle makes us feel tense and irritable. We become overexcited and emotionally disturbed. We are not able to concentrate on anything – this is because we are not in the present moment as our thoughts are either in the past or the future. So, the antidote is to bring us into the present moment. This is accomplished through breathing meditation or scanning what's happening in our body. This meditation will put us in a better frame of mind to continue. Also, if we are anxious about something, we need to find out why, because then we can start to change.

Doubt means the mind is filled with questions and uncertainties: Am I doing the right thing? Is my practice good? Will I be able to cultivate a calm mind? Am I wasting my time? The Buddha describes the mind filled with doubt as a pool of troubled water.

The simplest and most effective antidote for doubt is to ask questions and read books to find answers. You may find books or Buddhist teachers who say that doubt is useless, and you should simply believe the teachers and not question them; I encourage you to question and dig – questioning what our teachers transmit to us can be a very useful exercise, but we must always question with the aim of better understanding and not to humiliate or discredit people. I think the important thing is to cultivate confidence in the practice and the journey; I often take the image of the taxi in a city that we do not know, we trust that the driver knows the destination and how to get there, same thing for the dhamma and our teachers/Buddha. When we take the time to examine where doubt lives in our life, and not considering it as a negative thing but more as a way for us to change, we can work this obstacle as a door to liberation.

The five hindrances are traditionally considered obstacles or hindrances that prevent us from seeing things as they are and practicing with a clear mind. But we must also learn to live with them. They may not be the best roommates, but in this light, we can view negative thoughts and feelings as incentives to practice. Chögyam Trungpa, a Tibetan Buddhist teacher, used to describe them as the manure that helps the crops to grow. We also have the antidotes that help us work through these obstacles and also rely on positive thoughts and feelings. They are also instruments for change when we use the right approach/perspective.

How to Meditate
Beginner

Meditation, sometimes called mindfulness, is a practice that is often linked to the Buddhist spiritual path. In fact, it is integral to the Buddhist path. Meditation dispels inner chatter, creating restful contemplation and the liberation that the Buddha teaches. There are also several benefits when you have a daily practice. No matter what your motivation is now, it is important to follow certain instructions to benefit as much as possible.

Some tips for having the best possible conditions
(*the essentials*)
It is important to have a space without distractions. This is a privilege that is unfortunately limited for you. A penitentiary does not give you many opportunities (except perhaps the sacred space). Do your best to try to have your own cell, perhaps when your roommate is working or in a program; otherwise early in the morning before they open the cells or after the last count in the evening if your roommate is not watching television or snoring too loudly.

Decide the time of your meditation. I suggest starting with five minutes at the beginning and gradually increasing the time. The important thing is the frequency of your practice and not the minutes as such. Stay with the time you have chosen. If you have a timer, that's ideal because you don't need to look at the clock on your television all the time. Close your eyes and focus on your breathing until your time is up.

Meditation itself

Sit on your bed (if you are on top, you can sit on your chair/stool), make sure your back is straight. An upright posture will help you focus on your breathing as you inhale and exhale naturally without effort. If you are sitting on a cushion (I would fold it in half since it is not very big, you could also use your towel if it's dry and you can stack it on the pillow), position your legs so that you are comfortable. You can lay them out in front of you or cross them below you. The important thing is that you keep a straight, relaxed posture.

To get an idea of the typical meditation posture (cushion or chair), you can rely on the drawings in the appendix at the end of the book. Of course, this is just what I recommend, and you can change it a little to make it more comfortable for you. The key thing is that you are stable and solid in your posture. You've probably seen people fold their hands in their lap with thumbs gently touching, or rest their hands on their knees with their fingers up or down while meditating – but don't worry if these positions are uncomfortable, because the important thing is to be able to clear your mind and to concentrate on your breathing.

Also, it's good to tilt your chin to direct your gaze slightly downward; you can either close your eyes or keep them open during meditation (I still suggest closing your eyes, at least at the beginning, to block visual distractions), it doesn't matter. Tilt your chin and head while looking down (eyes open or not) to help open the chest and facilitate breathing.

Set your dial/timer when you are seated in an upright and comfortable position and ready to meditate. As I have already suggested, taking a shorter, realistic timeframe is a better way to begin to build and continue your practice – it is important not to put so much on your plate that you become discouraged and fail to continue. Also, you should not put too much pressure on yourself to reach a transcendental state after a week of practice. In fact, the beneficial effects of meditation can be very subtle so don't expect dramatic revelations. You want to build a practice gradually that has a good foundation that is solid and stable. This is why I say that starting with five minutes is perfect. Think of a house that is being built: start with the foundation one brick at a time.

Focus on your breathing; Meditation relies heavily on breathing. Instead of trying not to think about the things that bother you every day, focus on something positive like your breathing. You focus your concentration on your inhalations and exhalations. You'll see quite quickly that all the thoughts that come from outside go away by themselves, no need to worry about them and try actively to ignore them. When you focus on your breathing, try to be as comfortable as possible; you let your attention settle where it is most comfortable, that is, the lungs expanding and contracting, the abdomen rising and falling, or the air passing through the nose. I've heard before that some people will focus on the sound of their breathing.

The goal is to be present in each breath, not to be able to describe it. I don't want you to worry about being able to remember how you felt or being able to explain every moment and experience in the future. Simply live each breath, in the present moment. When one breath has passed, live the next one completely. You should not think about this breathing with your mind; you must simply experience it through your senses.

If your attention wanders, simply bring it back to your breathing, without judgment. Sometimes the thoughts that will take you away from the present moment are related to your family, your sentence, your transfer, your sense of security, and so on. The important thing is that you continually return to the present moment and the current breathing. If it's still difficult, you can always just focus on inhaling rather than exhaling; or perhaps it's easier to feel the breath leaving the body – the important thing is to find small solutions to facilitate concentration. I also know people who will count their breaths when it's too difficult to stay with the present moment. Many experienced meditators still do that after years of practice!

Meditation is not always easy. There will be days when things go well and other days not – this is why we say meditation is a practice. Don't be too hard on yourself, especially if you're a beginner. Over time you will build your meditative muscle – being mindful is a lifelong goal.

How to Build an Altar in a Cell

Buddhists have an altar in their homes, and many will also meditate in front of their altars. The altar serves as a focus of Buddhist religious ritual and as a place for profound contemplation. The offerings placed on the altar are an expression of the practitioner's devotion to the principle of enlightenment.

I'm sure you've seen beautiful altars on television or in books; but in prison one must always focus on the essential – this in no way detracts from the value of your altar in your cell. Your altar is as sacred as the one in any sacred space, or even in various temples; because every altar is a physical representation and reminder of the qualities one wants to develop. In addition, it can also serve as a focus for offerings, doing purification rituals, and so on – we will then not diminish its importance based on its looks or how extravagant (or not) it may be.

So where to put the altar? At home one has the privilege of being able to create a small sanctuary in a quiet room that gets lots of sunlight, for example. There are people who can even afford to reserve an entire room for the altar, because it is recommended not to have too many things in the room. Perhaps it is in a bedroom – but sometimes there is no choice and that's okay. My suggestion is to use your highest shelf, the one where most people have their TVs (you can always put that on your table) because it is high and away from other things, which ensures a clear and quiet space in your cell.

How to set up the altar? Are you wondering where to put everything?

An altar typically has symbols of the body, speech, and mind of the Buddha. The statue (if your penitentiary does not allow you to have a statue due to security concerns, your spiritual care worker will be able to validate everything with you) is the symbol of the body of the Buddha. Altars always have a statue or image (one of the images at the end of this book, a painting, or maybe little card/postcard that the Buddhist chaplain might be able to offer you) of Shakyamuni Buddha in the center; you can add other Buddhas or bodhisattvas or ancestors, but they are always put to the sides – the Buddha is always the central figure because everything comes from Buddha.

Afterwards, on the right side of the Buddha, then on the left when you look at your altar, you put Dhamma texts (such as the *Heart Sutra*, included in the back of this book). You can always change to another text if it speaks to you more; the important thing is that they are suttas[17] that the Buddha would have pronounced. The text represents the discourse of the Buddha.

And then on the left side of the Buddha, the right when you face your altar, we have a stupa[18] which

---

17 Sutta, Pali. Sutra, Sanskrit.

18 Stupa, Pali and Sanskrit. Chorten, Tibetan. Pagoda, Chinese,

represents the mind of the Buddha. There is a picture in the back of this book of the Mahabodhi temple at Bodhi Gaya, that is the spot where Shakyamuni Buddha attained Enlightenment.

I know you might want to have a more elaborate altar like you see in temples where they can afford to have representations of the three main lineages. But since there may be cell searches and security standards vary depending on the penitentiary, it is sometimes more prudent to keep everything as essential and simple as possible to prevent objects from being mistreated or broken. (During cell searches a Chaplain or Elder should be present to handle all sacred objects – to ensure that it is all done with respect and care). In fact, this type of minimalism is highly prized in the Zen traditions, where less is more. When you are out, you can decide on an altar that more represents your vision.

Now that your altar is set up, you can allow yourself to really stop and look at your altar from time to time during the day, especially if you are having a difficult time or feel agitation and big emotions. You may be feeling like you are drowning in bad emotions, and you see your Buddha sitting there – calm, so calm, even in this tornado of emotions. In this moment, remember that you too can be like this; hoping that this realization will help bring out that calm energy that resides within you.

Korean, or Japanese.

Buddhist Diet

While serving time in the penitentiary, food is important and there may be exceptions based on religious and moral beliefs, but all requests must be explored before being accepted or refused. Vegetarianism has become a much more common diet; several reasons are given – religion, moral conviction for the treatment of animals, the environment, or even simply health. But, regarding Buddhism, it is not necessarily the case that all Buddhists are vegetarians or vegan.

Why do people think all Buddhists are vegetarians? I must admit that I don't know why. It's probably based on the image that we are sold of Buddhism in the general culture here in the West. Many people also believe that the decrees of King Ashoka (257 BCE), an Indian Buddhist king who is honored in both Theravada and Mahayana schools, mention the prohibition of animal sacrifice and a commitment to vegetarianism.

For Theravadins this is not really the case, because monks are instructed to accept with equanimity and gratitude whatever is offered by villagers on their alms run every morning. This means that the food offered could include meat; they should not be refusing the generosity of the people who support them – it would not be appropriate. However, this does not mean that many Buddhists do not consume a vegetarian diet.

Sometimes we mix cultural and religious practices; This does not mean that culture cannot influence religion or vice versa. Yes, in ancient India, most people were vegetarians. Meat was for the rich.

This historical or cultural context may not be the reason why we may want to become vegetarian in line with our Buddhist beliefs. Often people will base their aspirations on the first precept we take when we become Buddhist. The first precept that we undertake to follow is that of "honoring life" or "not killing/taking life". It's true – becoming vegetarian seems like an easy way to reduce the lives taken on our plate. As for me, when I became a Buddhist and took refuge, I was already a vegetarian for reasons of moral conviction for just treatment of animals. My decision was already made, so it was not a big change for me. If you are meditating on being vegetarian as a Buddhist, the question you are asking yourself is legitimate, but it does not need to be answered immediately.

I encourage you to meditate on this question. What I like most about the precepts is that they are not rigid and can change throughout our practice and journey. The reason I also encourage it is that your situation is different from that of someone outside who makes the same decision. Here a vegetarian diet will be questioned, analyzed with a certain suspicion, and perceived as a privilege (even if this is not the case in my eyes). Anything that takes you out of the group is a privilege. When you eat vegetarian in the penitentiary you have to remember that there will be less variety (plenty of guys have told me that there were chickpeas way too often), your canteen will be revised (so if you buy animal products to repay a debt that is problematic; we all know that it is not allowed to accumulate debts but we know that it still is a common practice), and also if it is observed that you never eat animal products (people on special diets rarely have access to a second course/service like those who eat on the line) – you could lose everything. I'm not saying this to be moralistic, because you can consume animal products and that doesn't take away your commitment to Buddhist practice; I'm not here to judge, but I prefer to be honest too. Yes, people who receive a diet of conscience or for religious reasons are expected to be perfect in their diets; It's not necessarily right, but it's the reality.

All that to say, take the time to think about it; continue to meditate and deepen your knowledge of Buddhist teachings. Living a life of compassion and wisdom may look different to different people; find your place on your spiritual path and support will come accordingly. In short, vegetarianism is not obligatory to be a Buddhist; you can spread compassion in other ways if you feel like it.

Sit in the Fire

An unfortunate reality of doing time is that our loved ones are also doing time in their own way, which can put a lot of stress on relationships. It can also make us lose our partners as the sentence is a reality too difficult for them to bear. Sometimes, not only does the relationship end, but your ex-partner will find someone else while you are still in prison, and you find out by accident or more suddenly than you would normally. This pain burns you up inside; the feeling of helplessness and having to simply witness it must be so difficult. This practice that I am about to share has helped me a lot in my difficult times, it's called "sitting in the fire."

The Buddha's first noble truth is that people experience dukkha, that feeling of dissatisfaction or suffering, that feeling that something is wrong. The emotions you feel from your breakup are pronounced (which is completely normal). When the pain is pronounced like it is right now, it's completely normal to turn to meditation to relieve it. But, as you soon realized, the meditation you were trying can't relieve the pain you are feeling – breathing meditation won't give you a break or mental calm. So, the best option/solution is to just sit in the middle of this pain (of your inner fire). Just sit for the whole time of meditation in the fire and try not to find a particular meditation to put out the fire – just sit there.

It's normal that during these moments you might feel like a little child sitting on a chair with your feet off the ground. Like you have experienced, ending a long-term relationship feels like losing your feet. This is where you need to understand that you need to learn to relax in the face of pain. It's normal that you want to avoid this place within yourself, that you feel that it hurts, that you are unloved, or that it is a pain that is unacceptable. So, you start to breathe, you realize that this is a pivotal moment (the story is changing, and it's a big change), you have to learn to get to the bottom of this pain – even if it can feel like death.

When you hit rock bottom in pain, you feel that you have misinterpreted the situation as something wrong with you. When you relax into this feeling, you can see how it flows through you and that you are not dead after all. It will go away; you understand that your resistance to the idea that you are not lovable only makes the pain worse.

Remember that there is nothing in your life that can serve as a basis for your spiritual practice. Your spiritual practice is your life, twenty-four hours a day – there's no escaping it. The reason you have your formal meditation practice is because it brings you closer to the states of mind that you experience in your life during times of crisis. So, when you practice meditation, you must not run away from what is happening to your body and mind; they are simply present moment experiences.

Over time, you may realize that turning toward your discomfort becomes a source of happiness.

Because when you avoid pain – you are locked in a cycle of suffering. The Buddha teaches that what you think is solid is not solid – it is fluid. It is a dynamic energy.

These difficult moments become like portals, doors that take us to a different state of mind. Typically, when you experience pain, your instinct to avoid it is often reinforced, or the pain leads to other habits rooted in the misconception that something is inherently wrong. However, if you fully embrace the experience, as I encourage you to do, it opens the door to what we call "a timeless now."

There is nothing wrong with your thoughts and emotions, but you identify with them and make them feel solid. But if you don't identify with them, you begin to see life as a kind of movie in which you are the main character. You need to let go of the script and have an immediate experience of what is really happening, without blaming yourself – or anyone else. So, you must not become addicted to the story ruminating in your mind. In this moment, as history constantly repeats itself, we lose our balance and our intelligence. But if you notice it happening, you can catch it and choose a different path—a new alternative. If you keep doing what you've always done, you'll never break free.

The best advice I can give you is to stay in the immediacy of the experience. The solution is to start breathing in and out. It doesn't have to be a big spiritual act, just something to replace your usual reaction. This ensures that if you don't have the usual response, the urge will pass, and you will move on to something else. Also, when you don't have the usual reaction, you see that there are at least two possible outcomes and your desire for the old outcome quietly disappears. I hope this will help you during difficult times, I know it can be very difficult,

Empty Boat

Anger is a very common emotion to be feeling in prison; the place is a fountain of possibilities for you to live frustration, disappointment, difficulties, and so on. I understand how some people have come to me to say that they eventually feel like everything seems to bother them and that they end up feeling angry all the time. After working in the prison system for many years, I have been able to witness just how difficult it must be to live on the various ranges – that it is pretty much impossible to be able to find a place to be alone and have some peace and quiet. This quest of escaping the chaos of range life for a perfect quiet and peaceful spot makes me think of the empty boat teaching:

> There is a monk who decides that he wants to meditate alone but he lives in a monastery, and it is not easy to find a place where he can be alone. Far from the monastery, he takes a boat and goes to the middle of the lake, he closes his eyes and begins to meditate. After a period of continuous silence and calm, he suddenly feels the blow of another boat hitting his.
>
> With his eyes still closed, he begins to feel his anger rise and invade his entire body. He opens his eyes to shout at the person who

just ran into him, this person who dared to disturb him in the middle of meditation! But when his eyes are opened, he only sees a single empty boat, unsecured and floating in the middle of the lake....

It is at this moment that the monk finally realizes and understands that anger is within him; all it takes is for an external object to trigger it. After this moment and this profound lesson, when someone irritates him or provokes his anger, he remembers that the other person is just an empty boat and that the anger is within him.

We like to blame our anger on external phenomena, unpleasant or uncomfortable people or circumstances, but the anger is still within us, and these factors are simply empty boats that hit us to disrupt it and make it arise in us.

During our outbursts of anger, our dialogue of indignation, and so on towards others or certain situations is a perfect time for us to remember this teaching. Can we let go of our attachment to the rope we have gripping the empty boat, look at our own boat and heal our own anger; for wrath resides in our boat and our boat only.

Personally, when I experience a situation where I experience anger, I gently tell myself "empty boat." A simple reminder, sometimes, a reminder that makes me laugh because I can see how I need to be kinder to myself in these moments. A simple little reminder like this can help avoid situations where our anger can make things worse and do irreparable damage. So, every time you feel that a person or a situation is disturbing and giving rise to anger – empty boat, it is only an empty boat which disturbs your inner peace by awakening the anger already present in you.

Slowing Down

I have had many conversations with people who struggled with the pace of life in prison versus what they were living outside before their arrest. It is true that outside we glorify busyness, like if a busy calendar is a marker of success; so, it is normal to feel the shock when we begin our sentence. The days are long, they all look alike, and mostly, there is nothing going on. The reception (the three-month initial evaluation) time of your sentence is a big moment of adjustment, not just because the sentence has become much more real and tangible but also you must learn to slow down from the pace of life you had outside. So how do you transition from a completely busy schedule to a completely free schedule?

It's not easy. Not all transitions in our lives are easy and it takes time to adjust. So, it should come as no surprise that the transition from life outside to life in the penitentiary is one of the most difficult you will go through in your life. When you were provincial you always had the hope of release without federal incarceration; your sentence was not known and true at a certain level – now the sentence is true, and we must prepare for our sentence. Long or not, everything is relative, two years is still a large period. We must not minimize the time imposed on us; we just must learn to make the best of that time. So, you had a busy lifestyle outside, which means that to have a good time you must learn to slow down....

Many of us like to be busy; we value a busy schedule – we glorify being busy above all else, but that's not necessarily what we should want. It's true that a busy, fast, busy pace of life can give us a feeling of accomplishment and success; but at the source, this is not necessarily the case. Learning to slow down is beneficial, but it is an art and practice. Often when we walk quickly to a destination, we may notice that we are already at our destination in our thoughts even if it is far from where we are in the moment.

Can we ensure that our mind does not leave our body when we move? When we walk, can we stay in our body? Feel the body moving, moving forward, the wind against our face, and so on.? When we take a shower, same thing: our attention on the body, the soap, the water that removes the soap, the perfumes, the temperatures, and so on?

So when we start to slow down, can we examine the inner imperative that makes us feel like we need to be busy? We feel the desire to create the "I" who does these activities? Can we just feel the qualities of the moment of movements? When we take the time to slow down and be present in the moment, we quickly realize our old need to be busy. Being calm and mindful are two of the fruits of Buddhist practice.

I know that time passes slowly when we are in reception, but when we are truly present, we find that each moment is full of experiences that are happening simultaneously and continuously.

The opinions of others

Being in prison can carry a certain stigma; unfortunately some people have a hard time getting away from the crimes that brought them to prison and feel like this moment in their lives will always follow them. It is completely normal to feel that there are more obstacles than anything else when we are incarcerated; and the opinions of others, or what we perceive as the opinions of others, can be a burden that is hard from which to free ourselves. Here is an example of the typical question I receive about the opinions of others:

> I have a lot of trouble with the way the staff (guards and staff) look at me; I feel judgment and they don't even know me. I tell myself it's going to be the same when I get out; these looks will follow me forever.

The opinions that others have about you are not your own, nor are they a reflection of who you are. I often say, "what other people think of me is none of my business," meaning that I have no control over how I am perceived by others. So, remember that how people treat you is not a reflection of who you are, but of them. Unfortunately, there's not much you can do to change their opinions; they are attached to rigid points of view which leave no room for change or openness – and it is still not you who is going to change these points of view by trying to convince them differently. Also, all of this energy is focused on just one part of your complete identity.

You may have already heard about intersectionality in social justice circles and causes. That concept also applies in this context: you are a person in the justice system, but also a father, a husband, a son, a colleague at your workplace, and so on. Yes, when you are in the penitentiary, people will focus a lot on one of your identities; but it is up to you to remember all the other identities that live within you. You are more than what brought you here, and it is thanks to these other identities that you will be able to remain a good person who always has something to offer to others.

So, yes, people will judge you and treat you unfairly. They will cling to their prejudices and judgments, without knowing you and all the causes and conditions that brought you here today – but those are their problems. I am not minimizing what you did, and I know that neither are you, but I firmly believe that when you have a more complete picture of someone, you have more empathy and understanding for their situation. Sometimes it's easier not to know a person if you want to judge them. I am sure that some of your own prejudices have been broken down with the guys that you have been doing your time with; you might be changing your mind on certain "types" of people as you have built a more personal relationship with them, to realize that we are more than just one thing.

When I started my practice, I thought that everyone around me had to change; with time and the wisdom I have accumulated, I realize that it is me who must change – because I am the only person I can control. The only thing you can do is be the best person you can be, and not be too hard on yourself too – there are enough other people judging you; you don't need to add to this choir of voice. The only thing that belongs to you in this life is your actions. So be the best person you can be in each moment and maybe your actions/behaviours will change some hearts and minds.

Angulimala

Stories of spiritual transformation can be inspiring; these stories can be very useful to us when we are going through a rough time. Hope can be a powerful thing; it can make you believe that change is possible and that things can be different – that if you do the work, you can experience some inner changes that will help you heal and move forward. I often get asked if there are stories that can be inspiring specially for prisoners.

I can't speak for other religions, but there is Angulimala, a Buddhist story that is used as a symbol of spiritual transformation – his story is a lesson where anyone can change their life for the better, even the least susceptible people.

Among Buddhists, Angulimala's story is one of the best-known. From a Buddhist perspective, Angulimala's story serves as an example that even the worst of people can overcome their flaws and return to the right path. It clearly shows how good karma can destroy bad karma. Buddhists widely view Angulimala as a symbol of complete transformation and as a showcase that the Buddhist path can transform even the least likely followers. Buddhists have elevated the story of Angulimala as an example of the Buddha's compassion and supernatural achievement. Angulimala's conversion is cited as a testimony to the Buddha's abilities as a teacher and as an example of the healing qualities of the Buddha's teaching (Dhamma).

Through his response, the Buddha connects the notion of "refraining from harm" to stillness, which is the cause and effect of not harming. Furthermore, the story illustrates that there is spiritual power in such stillness, as the Buddha is described as surpassing the violent Angulimala. Although this is explained as being the result of the Buddha's supernatural achievement, the deeper meaning is that the spiritually resolute person can move more quickly than the conventionally active person. In other words, spiritual fulfillment is only possible through nonviolence. Furthermore, this stillness refers to the Buddhist notion of liberation from karma: if one cannot escape the endless law of karmic retribution, one can at least reduce one's karma by practicing non-violence.

Angulimala's story illustrates how criminals are affected by their psychosocial and physical environments. Many believe that someone begins to kill because their moral system collapses. The attitude could be summed up as follows: "I have no value; therefore, I can kill. If I kill, it proves that I have no value." Summarizing the life of Angulimala, we can say that he is a figure who bridges the gap between giving and taking life. Similarly, referring to the psychological concept of moral injury, we can describe Angulimala as someone who is betrayed by an authority figure but manages to regain his eroded moral code and repair his relationship with the community his actions have affected. Survivors of moral injury need a clinician and a community of people who face challenges together but deal with them safely; similarly, Angulimala is able to recover from his moral injury due to the Buddha as spiritual guidance and to a monastic community that leads a disciplined life, tolerant of difficulties. Angulimala's story could be used as a kind of narrative therapy and describes the ethics presented in the story as an inspiring responsibility. The story is not about being saved, but rather about saving yourself with the help of others.

Many people have written about the story of Angulimala and its implications for the justice system. They believe that in Buddhist ethics the only reason offenders should be punished is to reform their character. So, if an offender, like Angulimala, has already reformed, there is no reason to punish him, even as a deterrent.

Many describe the story of Angulimala as the first concept of transformative or restorative justice. This is demonstrated with Angulimala, his blanket renunciation of his former life as a bandit, and the forgiveness he ultimately receives from the relatives of his victims.

Here is the story of Angulimala:

> Buddhist scriptures report that one day, after his meal, the Buddha left the monastery where he was staying and headed towards a large forest. Seeing him going in this direction, various people working in their fields called him to warn him that in this forest lived the dreaded Angulimala.

Little is known about Angulimala, but the usual account of his life makes him the son of a wealthy family and at one time a brilliant student at the ancient University of Taxila in northwestern India.

At Taxila, other students were jealous of him and managed to poison their teacher's mind against him, so that the teacher asked him to pay what he would surely believe to be an impossible graduation fee: a thousand little human fingers of the right hand. Incredibly, instead of giving up and quietly going home without graduating, the young man proceeded to gather those fingers and pay the fee. Presumably he soon discovered that people were reluctant to willingly give up their little fingers and so he was forced to resort to violence and murder to obtain them.

Then he discovered he had nowhere to put those fingers. He tried to hang them on a tree, but the birds stole them, so his solution was to put them around his neck. For this gruesome and growing garland of bloody fingers, he was nicknamed Angulimala, meaning "garland of fingers" or "necklace of fingers".

This was the man who, looking out from his den, saw the Buddha approaching him, and who that day had nine hundred and ninety-nine little fingers around his neck. This powerful and athletic serial killer, who had already successfully resisted several attempts to apprehend him, grabbed his weapons and rushed to assassinate the Buddha and complete his score.

Angulimala expected to overtake him easily and quickly complete the work, but a very strange thing happened – even though the Buddha was only walking, serene and unhurried, Angulimala, despite his formidable strength and speed, realized he couldn't catch up. Finally, exhausted, angry, frustrated and drenched in sweat, Angulimala shouted at the Buddha to stop.

Then the Buddha turned around and, without anger or fear, speaking calmly and directly, he told Angulimala that he, the Buddha, had already stopped. He had stopped killing and harming and now it was time for Angulimala to do the same. Angulimala was so struck by these words that he stopped immediately; he threw down his weapons and followed the Buddha to the monastery where he became a monk.

Later, the king, unaware of what had happened, came leading his troops to arrest Angulimala. Being a very pious monarch, he called to pay homage to the Buddha and inform him of what he was doing. The Buddha asked the king what his reaction would be if he discovered that among this assembly of monks sat Angulimala.

To the king it was quite incredible that such a crude and perverse person could now be a Buddhist monk and sit among such exalted company, but if that were the case, he replied, he would certainly pay homage and would make offerings. Then the Buddha stretched out his right hand and, pointing, announced that Angulimala was seated just there.

When he had mastered his fear and recovered from the shock, the king, after paying homage, told the Buddha how incredible it was that "What we tried to do by force and with weapons, you you did without force or weapons!" Over time, after a period of trials for himself, Angulimala finally succeeded in purging his mind of all greed, hatred and delusion, and realized for himself the Buddhist goal of Enlightenment.

The story of Angulimala teaches us that the possibility of Enlightenment can be awakened in the most extreme circumstances, that people can and do change, and that people are best influenced by persuasion and especially by example.

The Power of Practice
(letter received from a prison resident)

Hi Samaneti,

Thank you very much for your teaching on Angulimala, even if this teaching dates back a long time – I find that it still speaks to me today. This is one thing that I really like about Buddhist teachings, they are timeless, and I find that they speak to me in my life. It was not the first time that you spoke to me about this mythical character, but the most recent time, when I returned to my cell, I took a moment to reflect on how this spiritual path is integral to many people who change their lives. During this reflection, I took a moment to think about mine (without sharing too much so people know who I am) and how Buddhism has helped me immensely – hoping that my sharing can help/encourage people to turn to this practice.

As you know, my childhood was not easy. I was a child from a modest family who would be bullied and ridiculed by children from financially well-off families. For many years I was psychologically and physically terrorized – rejection took its toll; destroyed, I withdrew into myself.

As a teenager, my family moved to a new neighbourhood – and it was there that I met a group young delinquents who accepted me as I was immediately.

We would commit little petty petty crimes repeatedly, I would tell myself that they were my true friends. As an adult, going in and out of prison, where I was around much bigger criminals, I started to tell myself that I wanted to become important like them.

I joined a gang of bank robbers who were very respected in the 'industry' – I told myself that with money I could have everything I wanted materially, in addition to respect and admiration since I had reached the criminal peak. I then started to take human lives for this organization, making me very important in its hierarchy – at least that's what I thought.

One day I asked myself the question if my criminal lifestyle was giving me the life I was supposed to have in my childhood? It was during this questioning that I realized that taking lives was becoming more and more difficult to live with everyday. As I analyzed my life it showed me the actions toward me by the people who were my so-called friends – lies and being frequently manipulated. I became more and more suspicious of them and no longer trusted them.

Since I had had bad experiences in the past, especially on the religious side, I told myself that no one could help me. I lived alone and withdrawn – silent and closed off from anyone who tried to help me after my incarceration – I thought people wanted me to open up to get something and not help me heal of my multiple traumas.

One day I observed from afar the actions and words of a Buddhist teacher who would come and visit in my sector of the prison. Very gradually my suspicions and wariness began to diminish. It's as if this person's teachings had just given me a sign – because at the beginning I told myself I needed to turn the page and begin healing to change – but I was still refusing to face the real things in front of me. But this teacher taught me not to run away from reality – to know how to say things honestly and take responsibility for them – to successfully break down the walls that protected me from reality brick by brick. To say things by their real names and to acknowledge them – which released deep emotions that I no longer had to hold in.

These teachings taught me that I could not change the past but that I could see my present life differently and create the causes and conditions for my future. I discovered a new world and saw that this new world had much more value than it once possessed – values that give meaning to my existence.

Today I love what I have become (even if I am still in prison). The spiritual side of Buddhism and meditation – this is the greatest gift for me. Thank you Samaneti for giving me all these ingredients to awaken a more positive vision of life. I also hope that my story will inspire others to follow in my footsteps and change their lives for the better.

Anonymous

Homage to Our Ancestors

We are the continuation of the Buddha, just as the student is the continuation of the teacher and the child the continuation of his parents. We have blood ancestors, and we also have spiritual ancestors. The Buddha is my spiritual ancestor – as are the centuries of lineage teachers and practitioners who followed him and kept these precious teachings alive. I was born from them, I am their continuation, I am them – in me they are alive.

I am the Buddha. I have accepted Siddhartha Gotama as my guide, but I am aware that besides him there are many other Buddhas. I also acknowledge that I am Ajahn Chah, I am Ajahn Buddhadasa, I am Shunryu Suzuki and all the thousands of teachers who have ensured that the teachings have survived for over 2,600 years and are now available to me. These teachers, these Buddhadhamma teachers, fought against oppression and attempts to silence them. Thanks to their efforts and struggles, we can study these precious teachings in our homes, across an ocean.

I bow in gratitude to all the people who came to my shores from Asia who built Buddhist communities (sometimes in secret out of fear of violence from my ancestors), who were instrumental in ensuring that these teachings would take root and thrive on these lands. I bow in humility for this gift of Dhamma, for their willingness to share its transformative practices and teachings so that I can benefit from them. Without my Dhamma ancestors, I would not have had these teachings and they would have been lost, instead of living and thriving for the benefit of all beings.

It is important that we connect with our Dhamma ancestors; we are their continuation. We must practice contact with our ancestors every day. Our altars honor them, as a point of contact between them and us. An example could be that we offer them incense every day – they do not smell the incense, but when we light the incense stick, we focus our attention on the presence of our ancestors. This is an opportunity to touch our ancestors within us. This can help us realize that our ancestors are still alive within us, because we are the continuation of our ancestors.

I take refuge in the Buddha
I take refuge with other Buddhas
I take refuge with the Bodhisattvas, the
    Mahasattvas
I take refuge with all the teachers and students
    who have helped Buddhism survive in its
    birthplace, Asia
I take refuge with all the people who brought
    these teachings to my shores
I take refuge with all my spiritual ancestors,
    followers of Buddhadhamma

How to meditate
More Experienced

Meditation allows people who practice Buddhism to evolve and overcome the distractions that present themselves, in order to penetrate the deeper nature of things. The effects of your practice are effective at many levels. For example, it is often said that meditation practice helps reduce blood pressure, stress, anxiety, depression, insomnia and even the aging of our brain. It also improves cognitive and emotional behaviors. Meditation on loving-kindness can help resolve your anger issues, your interpersonal conflicts (love, family, and friends). This practice that we often call metta is essential for a balanced practice. I will explain the basic meditation again (a little more quickly since I already did it for beginner meditation), then I will also briefly discuss the obstacles you may have during your meditations and finish my instructions with a *metta* practice – an important practice for your heart and mind.

You choose your preferable time for your meditation; some people like to meditate while getting up (this can be a good time, before lunch service and while most people are still sleeping, which helps cultivate a calm and quiet environment with less movement) or while going to bed (kind of the same concept, except that people are active and getting ready to go to bed, but you might have noise from the televisions in their cells); It's really up to you to choose what's best for you. There is no best time for me, they all have benefits (evening meditation can help us sleep better, but a morning practice also helps us start the day calmer and more balanced). Really choose what works best for you. If you don't know, try one week in the morning and one week in the evening and you can make a more informed decision.

Ideally, it is best to meditate when you are not tired; but this may not always be the case. I know that at reception there are a lot of guys who are not getting refills for the sleeping pills that they had at the provincial level; this has a huge disruptive factor on their sleep. You must stay kind to yourself. Also, it's not easy being inside (separated from your family, making peace with your crimes and the work you must do in relation to your risk factors, and so on) and difficulty in falling asleep is quite actually normal.

After you have chosen the best time for our practice, assume a comfortable seated posture (either on our bed or our chair/stool). The classic posture for meditation is to cross your legs in front of you, hands resting on your knees or folded in your lap – but if this is not comfortable and you spend your entire meditation moving, try to find a position that is sustainable. Just ensure that your your back is always straight and that you have a posture worthy of the practice.

The main thing is that you are comfortable and can breathe fully and deeply.

Relax your body; by having the correct posture where you can stay comfortable and relaxed when you meditate. Tilt your head forward slightly, if you feel safe you can close your eyes (if this is too difficult, you can keep them half open and look down at the floor) and do your best to keep your chest open to make breathing easier. You can also put your tongue in contact with your palate and swallow your saliva. Your suction will also help reduce your amount of saliva, as well as the need to swallow.

Focus on your breathing; breathe through your nose; focus on each inhale and exhale. I am always attentive to my abdomen which swells and hollows (which rises and falls); I am simply aware of my breathing, without trying to control it. No need to place your attention on the abdomen if you are used to observing the rib cage or the nose; the important thing is to stay where you are most comfortable. Stay focused on your breath. The goal is to achieve a certain peace and stillness of your mind.

Let your thoughts come and go. It is inevitable that thoughts will arrive in your mind, especially in the beginning, but they never leave completely – it is more their volume that changes with time and experience. You don't want to stop your thoughts, you let them happen, you realize their presence, but you don't feed them (as I often tell you, you let the bus pass but you don't get on it). The goal is not to stop thinking, but to make the thoughts become powerless. Thoughts must leave our minds of their own accord. Meditation is not just the search for inner peace (although this is still a very important aspect); it is a practice that helps us to see deeply and to see what is happening beneath the surface.

Aside from recurring thoughts and feelings, there are also other obstacles you will face that can complicate your meditation such as pain from prolonged sitting, a desire to sleep, cravings, or other things.

So, what can you do when you experience these things?

Pain: if you are not comfortable, you do not move. You review your body and the pain, you explore the sensation, you imagine that your body is an empty vessel and that you are outside. If the pain is too intense, you can get up to take a short break or move gently to ease your pain – but always observing the sensations with your movement.

Craving: You may have times when it is difficult to put aside your desires to think about lovers or objects that you desire. You must remain aware that cravings are fleeting, if you satisfy one – another will appear. You can think about the substance of the object of your desires: remember that a body is simply skin, bones and flesh.

Lack of sleep or preoccupation: you notice your feelings, without fueling them. You redirect your attention to your breathing or the movements of your abdomen. If a thought is stubborn and you can't get rid of it, you can write a short note that will serve as a reminder for you to worry about the problem later.

Drowsiness/fatigue: you try to remember your reasons for meditating. You can also focus on imagining a white light between your eyebrows to increase your alertness. If you realize that the fatigue is too much, you can wash your face with cold water or meditate while standing – but if it continues, it may be better to take a short nap and try again later.

Over time, it's good to increase the length of your meditations. Start with five-minute sessions, once a day. At first, the five minutes will seem long and go by too slowly – but, as you progress, you will find the time easier. You will then try to increase in increments of five minutes, this can go up to when you have 20-30 minutes if you want. The important thing is to increase gradually.

The Practice of Metta

Loving kindness is an integral part of our Buddhist practice. It is a practice that aims to train our minds to show more kindness and more compassion. There is another section where I explain more about metta. In this section are some specific meditations on metta.

With this practice we try to develop a feeling of loving kindness towards:

- Ourselves;
- A loved one that we respect (example perhaps a spiritual guide);
- A loved one (it's best to start with someone we are not sexually attracted to);
- A neutral being towards whom we do not have any specific feelings;
- A hostile being (I sometimes like to think of this person more as a difficult person since a kind love for someone hostile may seem complicated now).

You begin this meditation after you have practiced mindful breathing (this will vary depending on the person meditating; what is important is that you feel that your mind has settled and has become more grounded and quieter). Therefore, when you find yourself in a more stable and deep state of contemplation and concentration, you can then try to send love and happiness first to yourself, and then spread these wishes to the other four types of people.

How do you bring about this feeling of loving kindness? There are three main techniques. The most popular technique is repeating simple phrases which cultivate this feeling of loving kindness; some people compare these phrases to mantras. For example:

> May I be happy and healthy.
> May I be calm and peaceful.
> May I be protected from all dangers.
> Make my mind stay away from hatred and
>   my heart be filled with love.

Of course, if these phrases don't do anything for you, you can always change the words so that you feel a connection to the words and wishes.

Visualization is another common technique. You create a mental image of yourself or the person you are thinking about. You visualize this person happy and smiling.

The last technique is reflection; you think about the good deeds and qualities of the person you are thinking about. You focus on the feeling, it's the emotion that counts, not the technique you choose to evoke it. When the feeling of loving kindness arises, you focus on it. When the feeling disappears, you return to the technique you used to evoke it.

You practice how to radiate a feeling of love; you project your feelings and your loving kindness towards the four cardinal points. It can be easier if you do it by thinking about the people you know who are in every direction you project your love. The goal is not just to spread love in this specific method, but simply to radiate a feeling of unconditional love everywhere.

For this love without limits and directions, you can recite phrases more suitable for this exercise.

For example:

I wish all human beings to be safe, happy,
    healthy, live in joy.
I wish all beings to be happy, safe, healthy,
    live in joy.

Do not forget, when you are able to radiate your loving kindness in all directions – you are sending it to all people. This includes your abusers, your oppressors, your victims, your cohabitants in prison (regardless of their charges or offenses), all incarcerated people (regardless of their charges or offenses), security agents, stakeholders (psychologists, maintenance workers, and social workers, parole officers), and so on. EVERYONE! When you can have a heart that is capable of radiating these wishes, you are free.

Walking Meditation

Walking meditation, commonly known as *kinhin* in the Japanese Zen tradition, is a meditation technique that involves walking while meditating. Normally our practice begins with sitting meditation, but sometimes we find it very difficult to meditate without moving if our mind is restless or busy – walking meditation can be very beneficial at times like this. Also, it is a good active way to integrate mindfulness into daily life. A practice that is frequent helps us feel grounded and balanced, so if it's too loud or disruptive in the pavilion or row – you can always go for a walk in the yard. The important thing is that you meditate and continue with the practice even with all the distractions present.

Most meditation techniques we see tell us to sit still, but walking meditation asks us to move the body, and work to bring the body and mind together to achieve emotional and physical balance. This technique is perfect for those who have difficulty sitting still during meditation sessions. If distractions from our normal location become too many or we have a lot of pain from sitting for too long, that change is good. It is really an excellent complement to sitting meditation.

So how do you meditate while walking? Before you start, you need to make sure you have enough space – that's why I recommend the courtyard. If the big courtyard is open that's better, because walking without distractions going to be much more complicated in the small courtyard. If you're doing it in your cell (which is possible too although eight feet isn't a lot of steps, so it can be a lot of walking back and forth which itself can become a distraction). Make sure your path isn't cluttered; that's why the big yard is perfect because you can just go around (or you can create a small track for yourself if it doesn't cause a problem with others walking).

Choose a foot, lift the foot, move it through the space and carefully place it on the floor in front of you. Feel the sensations of each part of the process, from heel to toe, and repeat with the other foot. This is a relaxed meditation. Don't forget to breathe; it will help you stay focused.

Make sure you walk with intention. You'll see quickly how you fall on autopilot (before my practice I was never aware of my feet, as if I was floating forward, like a force pushing me into the direction I wanted). I know it sounds weird at first to do it with this intention – but it's important if you want to take advantage of the walking practice. You will walk freely but consciously.

You should allow yourself to notice, become aware of your feet touching the ground, and pay attention to the physical sensations that pass through your body during each step (it could even be the wind brushing against your arms or legs). This helps you engage in the present moment while your body moves. Just acknowledge the sensations as you walk without judgment.

Sense your surroundings, take a broad sense of the environment around you – notice if the air touching your body is hot or cold, ambient sounds of birds, others around you, and so on. Is there a scent in the air? Taking this inventory of small details will help you walk mindfully.

Notice if your mind wanders or gets lost in its stories. If this is the case, bring your attention back to your breath and the sensation of your legs and your feet in contact with the ground, a continual return if necessary. The important thing is that you come back to the present moment – without judgment and always remaining kind to yourself. Over time, the practice will become easier. Throughout the physical experience you will dive deeper into a meditative state.

People often ask me about how fast to walk. Fast or slow may vary, but whatever pace allows you to be most present is best. Pace varies from one person to another. In Vietnamese and Japanese Soto Zen traditions, the walking is very slow. In Japanese Rinzai Zen, it is almost running. You can play with your pace and try not to focus too much on your speed. Hoping that this practice becomes a new opportunity to practice and be in the present moment on a more continuous basis.

Buddhist Festivals

Like all religions and spiritual paths, Buddhism has festivals throughout the year. The holidays vary depending on the tradition. Here is a basic list of the various holidays that you may like to highlight during the year. I tried to only share the holidays that are more widely celebrated throughout the Buddhist world. If you deepen your practice and want to specially deepen cultural practices for a specific lineage of Buddhism, you can always reach out to your regional Buddhist representative for other holidays specific to your lineage. Certain accommodations can be made for celebrations; it is important to consult with your Buddhist or site spiritual care worker to find out what is possible depending on the security level where you are. In prison, we sometimes have to make do with the minimum, not all sites will be as accommodating as they should be – this is a great opportunity for us to practice letting go and renewing our resolve to being patient and tolerant when we are faced with difficulties.

Mahayana (*China, Japan, Korea, Vietnam*)
January – Lunar New Year – first day after the new moon.
February 15 – Nehan-e (Nirvana Day) the memorial of the death of the Buddha.
April 8 – Buddha's Birthday.

August 26 – Jizo Day – Jizo (*aka* Ksitigharba) is the
Bodhisattva who is the savior of suffering beings
in the underworld, and he is also the protector of
children and the patron of deceased.

December 8 – Bodhi Day, celebration of the
awakening of the Buddha.

Theravada *(Sri Lanka, India, Bangladesh, Thailand,
Myanmar, Cambodia, Laos)*

February 5 – Magha (Sangha Day) commemorates
the spontaneous gathering of 1,250 arahants
(awakened monks) where the Buddha taught the
basis of the discipline.

April – Theravada New Year. Three-day celebration
after the first full moon in April.

May – Vesak – the most important day of the year
for all Buddhists. A commemoration of the birth,
awakening, and death of Buddha. Always on
the first full moon of May. Known as Wesak in
Mahayana and Saga Dawa in Vajrayana.

July – Asalha Puja (Dhamma Day) celebrated on the
July full moon, a celebration of the Buddha's first
discourse, which he gave to five monks at Deer
Park.

Vajrayana *(Tibet, Bhutan, Nepal, India, China, Japan)*

1st full moon in February – Losar (Tibetan New
Year).

July 6 – His Holiness the Dalai Lama's birthday.

Further Reading

Here are a few suggestions for further reading. These are my recommendations, and you may want to check with your Buddhist representative to see if there are other books that could be better suited for you and your studies. Be curious, read whatever books speak to you, let them inspire you to be better and more dedicated to your practice and path.

Stephen Batchelor
- *Buddhism without Beliefs: A Contemporary Guide to Awakening*
- *Confession of a Buddhist Atheist*

Bhikkhu Bodhi
- *The Noble Eightfold Path: Way to the End of Suffering*
- *Noble Truths, Noble Path: The Heart Essence of the Buddha's Original Teachings*

Buddhadasa Bhikkhu
- *Heartwood of the Bodhi Tree: The Buddha's Teaching on Voidness*
- *Seeing with the Eye of the Dhamma: The Comprehensive Teaching of Buddhasa Bhikkhu*

Ajahn Chah
- *Food for the Heart: The Collected Teachings of Ajahn Chah*
- *Being Dharma: The Essence of the Buddha's Teachings*

Pema Chödrön

- *When Things Fall Apart: Heart Advice for Difficult Times*
- *The Places That Scare You: A Guide to Fearlessness I Difficult Times*

Jack Kornfield

- *A Path with Heart: A Guide Through the Perils and Promises of Spiritual Life*
- *After the Ecstasy, the Laundry: How the Heart Grows Wise on the Spiritual Path*
- *The Wise Heart: A Guide to the Universal Teachings of Buddhist Psychology*

Stephen Levine

- *A Gradual Awakening*
- *A Year to Live: How to Live This Year as If It Were Your Last*

Jarvis Jay Master

- *That Bird Has My Wings: The Autobiography of an Innocent Man on Death Row*
- *Finding Freedom: Writings from Death Row*

Shunryu Suzuki

- *Zen Mind, Beginner's Mind*

Thich Nhat Hanh

- *The Heart of the Buddha's Teaching: Transforming Suffering into Peace, Joy, and Liberation*
- *Anger: Wisdom for Cooling the Flames*
- *Peace Is Every Step: The Path of Mindfulness in Everyday Life*

The Insight that Brings Us to the Other Shore (*Heart Sutta*)[19]

Translation by Thich That Hanh

Avalokiteshvara while practicing deeply with the Insight that Brings Us to the Other Shore, suddenly discovered that all of the five Skandhas are equally empty, and with this realization he overcame all Ill-being.

Listen Sariputra, this Body itself is Emptiness and Emptiness itself is this Body. This Body is not other than Emptiness and Emptiness is not other than this Body. The same is true of Feelings, Perceptions, Mental Formations, and Consciousness.

Listen Sariputra, all phenomena bear the mark of Emptiness; their true nature is the nature of no Birth, no Death, no Being, no Non-being, no Defilement, no Purity, no Increasing, no Decreasing.

That is why in Emptiness, Body, Feelings, Perceptions, Mental Formations and Consciousness are not separate self entities.

The Eighteen Realms of Phenomena which are the six Sense Organs, the six Sense Objects, and the

---

19 *The Insight that Brings us to the Other Shore* translation by Tich Nhat Hanh (2014) is licensed under a Creative Commons Attribution-NonCommercial 4.0 International License.

six Consciousnesses are also not separate self entities.

The Twelve Links of Interdependent Arising and their Extinction are also not separate self entities.

Ill-being, the Causes of Ill-being, the End of Ill-being, the Path, insight and attainment, are also not separate self entities.

Whoever can see this no longer needs anything to attain.

Bodhisattvas who practice *The Insight that Brings Us to the Other Shore* see no more obstacles in their mind, and because there are no more obstacles in their mind, they can overcome all fear, destroy all wrong perceptions, and realize Perfect Nirvana.

All Buddhas in the past, present and future, by practicing *The Insight that Brings Us to the Other Shore* are all capable of attaining Authentic and Perfect Enlightenment.

Therefore Sariputra, it should be known that *The Insight that Brings Us to the Other Shore* is a Great Mantra, the most illuminating mantra, the highest mantra, a mantra beyond compare, the True Wisdom that has the power to put an end to all kinds of suffering. Therefore let us proclaim a mantra to praise *The Insight that Brings Us to the Other Shore*:

Gate, Gate, Paragate, Parasamgate, Bodhi Svaha!
Gate, Gate, Paragate, Parasamgate, Bodhi Svaha!
Gate, Gate, Paragate, Parasamgate, Bodhi Svaha!

The Buddha's Words on Loving-Kindness (*Karaniya Metta Sutta*)

translated from the Pali by the Amaravati Sangha

This is what should be done.
By one who is skilled in goodness,
And who knows the path of peace:
Let them be able and upright,
Straightforward and gentle in speech,
Humble and not conceited,
Contented and easily satisfied,
Unburdened with duties and frugal in their ways.
Peaceful and calm and wise and skillful,
Not proud or demanding in nature.
Let them not do the slightest thing.
That the wise would later reprove.
Wishing: In gladness and in safety,
May all beings be at ease.
Whatever living beings there may be.
Whether they are weak or strong, omitting none,
The great or the mighty, medium, short or small,
The seen and the unseen,
Those living near and far away,
Those born and to-be-born —
May all beings be at ease!

Let none deceive another,
Or despise any being in any state.
Let none through anger or ill-will.
Wish harm upon another.
Even as a mother protects with her life.
Her child, her only child,
So with a boundless heart
Should one cherish all living beings.
Radiating kindness over the entire world:
Spreading upwards to the skies,
And downwards to the depths.
Outwards and unbounded,
Freed from hatred and ill-will.
Whether standing or walking, seated or lying down.
Free from drowsiness,
One should sustain this recollection.
This is said to be the sublime abiding.
By not holding to fixed views,
The pure-hearted one, having clarity of vision,
Being freed from all sense desires,
Is not born again into this world.

Meal Time Prayer

This food is the gift of the whole universe,
Each morsel is a sacrifice of life,
May I be worthy to receive it.
May the energy in this food,
Give me the strength,
To transform my unwholesome qualities
into wholesome ones.
I am grateful for this food,
May I realize the Path of Awakening,
For the sake of all beings.
The joys and pains of all beings
are present in the gift of this food.
Let us receive it in love
and gratitude...
And in mindfulness of our sisters and brothers
among living beings of every kind
who are hungry or homeless,
sick or injured,
or suffering in any way.

Author Unknown

Metta Prayer

May all beings be happy, contented and safe.
May every living creature, without any exception,
Whether moving or still,
Whether large, tall or medium, tiny or considerable,
Whether visible or invisible, living near or far,
Whether born or unborn, may all these creatures be
    happy.
May no one in any place disappoint or despise anoth-
    er.
May no one, out of anger or hatred, wish harm to
    another.
As a mother at the risk of her life, watches over and
    protects her only child,
Let me see others through an open mind,
May I love the creatures of the whole world without
    limits,
Above, below and all around,
Without limitation or hindrance, without harm or
    hostility.
Standing or walking, sitting or lying down, as long as
    I am awake,
Let me cultivate these thoughts.

Lao Tzu's Peace Prayer

If there is to be peace in the world,
There must be peace in the nations.
If there is to be peace in the nations,
There must be peace in the cities.
If there is to be peace in the cities,
There must be peace between neighbours.
If there is to be peace between neighbours,
There must be peace in the home.
If there is to be peace in the home,
There must be peace in the heart.

Bodhisattva Prayer
for Humanity

May I be a guard for those who need protection
A guide for those on the path
A boat, a raft, a bridge for those who wish to cross
    the flood
May I be a lamp in the darkness
A resting place for the weary
A healing medicine for all who are sick
A vase of plenty, a tree of miracles
And for the boundless multitudes of living beings
May I bring sustenance and awakening
Enduring like the earth and sky
Until all beings are freed from sorrow
And all are awakened.

Shantideva, Indian Buddhist sage, 700 CE.
(Prayer performed each morning
by His Holiness the Dalai Lama)

Prayer for the happiness and salvation of your family and friends

May I remain in joy, well-being and peace.
May my teachers remain in joy, well-being and peace.
May my parents remain in joy, well-being and peace.
May my relatives remain in joy, well-being and peace.
May my friends remain in joy, well-being and peace.
May strangers remain in joy, well-being and peace.
May hostile people remain in joy, well-being and
    peace.
May my enemies remain in joy, well-being and peace.
May all beings remain in joy, well-being and peace.

Generating the Four Immeasurables

May all beings be happy,
May all be free from suffering,
May no one ever be separated from happiness,
May all possess equanimity, free from hatred,
and attachment.

Traditional Buddhist Prayer

May all beings have happiness and the causes of
    happiness;
May all be free from sorrow and the causes of sor-
    row;
May all never be separated from the sacred happiness
    which is sorrowless;
And may all live in equanimity, without too much
    attachment and too much aversion,
And live believing in the equality of all that lives.

Author Unknown

Generating Bodhichitta

May I, through the virtues I accumulate through
    giving and other perfections,
Become a Buddha for the benefit of all. (3x)

Acknowledgments

I would first like to thank all the men and women I met in the various penitentiaries where I worked; you inspired me to write this book for you. Thank you.

I would like to thank my colleagues Drenpa and Akutobhaya, Buddhist spiritual care workers across Canada. Our conversations over the years have nourished these pages, planting seeds that have blossomed into this little book.

I thank my teachers Venerable Pannavati and Venerable Pannadipa; their wisdom and teachings are a gift that must be shared and spread within the walls – for these teachings are a map to the liberation of our hearts and minds. Happiness does not diminish in value if we share it.

I would like to thank Karma Yönten Gyatso and Brigitte Robert for editing to help these pages better. Thank you for all your work that was done in the spirit of *dana*; may the merit of your work help those reading these pages find liberation. Gratitude to Sumeru Press Inc. for publishing this book for the benefit of those incarcerated.

Thanks to my writing coach Josh Bartok, whose advice helped create the book you have in your hands right now.

Thank you to my partner for her support during this creative period.

Thank you to my *kalyanamittas*, my friends on the Buddhist path, my chosen sangha. You know who you are – without you this path would be very lonely and difficult.

Acharya Samaneti

Acharya Samaneti is a prison spiritual care worker, philosopher, lover of the written word and seeker of truth. The contemplative life called him very early in his life; an only child, Samaneti found comfort in silence, reflection, and personal inquiry. Samaneti wishes to bear witness to the universality of suffering and actions of love that awaken hearts. This mission leads him to work with incarcerated people and other marginalized populations.

The Three Jewels
All Buddhists take refuge in the Three Jewels
for guidance on the path:

1. Buddha (the exemplar)
2. Dhamma (the teachings)
3. Sangha (the community of practitioners)

The Four Noble Truths
The first and foundational teaching by the Buddha
about the nature of our experience and
our spiritual potential:

1. The existence of dukkha
2. The origin of dukkha
3. The cessation of dukkha
4. The path for the cessation of dukkha

The Noble Eightfold Path
The path the Buddha taught to those
seeking liberation/enlightenment:

1. Right View
2. Right Intention
3. Right Speech
4. Right Action
5. Right Livelihood
6. Right Effort
7. Right Mindfulness
8. Right Concentration

Five Precepts
Standards of conduct that are the
foundation of an ethical life

Refrain from:
1. Killing
2. Stealing
3. Sexual Misconduct
4. False, Harsh, Idle Speech
5. Intoxicants That Cloud the Mind

Six Sense Doors and Three Feeling Tones
Everything you experience comes through these doors:

1. Eye (seeing)
2. Ear (hearing)
3. Nose (smelling)
4. Tongue (tasting)
5. Body (touching)
6. Mind

Experience is felt as one of these tones
1. Pleasant
2. Unpleasant
3. Neutral

The Four Brahma-Viharas
The four sublime attitudes reflect
the mind state of enlightenment:

1. Loving Kindness (Metta)
2. Compassion (Karuna)
3. Joy (Mudita)
4. Equanimity (Upekkha)

Four Metta Phrases

The four traditional phrases or words that are
traditionally used to send loving kindness
to all living beings:

1. May I be free from danger
2. May I be happy
3. May I be healthy
4. May I be at ease

The Six Stages of Metta

Your circles of living beings that you
expand your wishes of loving kindness:

1. Yourself
2. A Good Friend
3. A Neutral Person
4. A Difficult Person
5. All Four
6. All Living Beings

Five Hindrances

The common hindrances to meditation practice:

1. Desire, clinging, craving
2. Aversion, anger, hatred
3. Sleepiness, sloth
4. Restlessness
5. Doubt

The Six Wholesome and Unwholesome Roots of Mind

1. Generosity
2. Love
3. Wisdom
4. Greed
5. Hatred
6. Delusion

The Three Kinds of Dukkha

The Buddha taught us that we can understand different kinds of dukkha through these categories:

1. The dukkha of pain
2. The dukkha of change
3. The dukkha of conditionality

The Three Marks of Existence

The Buddha discovered three universal truths that all things have. They are:

1. Annica (impermanent – everything in life is impermanent, always changing)
2. Dukkha (unsatisfactory – because nothing is permanent, a life based on possessing things doesn't make you happy)
3. Anatta (no soul – there is no eternal unchanging self, we are a collection of changing characteristics or attributes)

www.ingramcontent.com/pod-product-compliance
Lightning Source LLC
La Vergne TN
LVHW091310080426
835510LV00007B/441